EXTRA MONEY
EXTRA POWER
EXTRA HAPPY
EXTRA EASY
- HELPFUL INSIGHT

By Anonymous Author

Hi and hello! You are now officially in control. Well to put it mathematicall y....

$$\text{Feel(Thoughts + Belief)} \times \text{(Naturalness\% + intensity\%)}$$

$$=$$

$$\text{Desire/Reality Imagination + Belief} = \text{Your World}$$

Welcome to HELPFUL INSIGHT
Extra Money
Extra Power
Extra Happy
Extra Easy…Simple life techniques to reach your

desire with guaranteed results...TIP: "Be decisive and clear on why and what/Then how, when, and where will automatically show up." IMAGINATION GUARANTEES THE LIFE YOU WANT; SO TAKING ACTION IS

EASY ON THE NERVES AND IS ALWAYS PROMISING GOOD RESULTS.This is where we get out of our own way and nature does the rest as it has since the beginning of time. Why are we not tapping into this nonstop success potential? One answer is because struggle is entertaining, what we've been taught as logical reality seems fair enough, and it's easy to think small. Negative emotions are easy to come by in a world of chaos. So we imagine more negative and then sure enough we keep experiencing the same chaos or boring blah over and over. It is ALWAYS OUR FAULT

BECAUSE WE ARE ALWAYS IN CONTROL. The world only has so much negative chaos because throughout history few knew and know just how easy it is to fix their world by positive emotional influence. That sounds too good to be true. Having a cell phone use to sound to good to be true. However with faith and action all desires come easy into existence. Many mentally insecure people are starting to taste this success and so should you! Live these few steps daily accessing your powerful control button and see constant results, all while feeling a sense of ease and being the one truly in charge. So what is this powerful control button I speak of? It is the believing what you imagine and wearing that feeling daily and nightly while ignoring what the physical world keeps telling you is true. Everything around you has already been imagined so it has already been created and you need not worry about it. You need to focus on what will be created next. Just keep starting to create by living what you imagine in your heart and mind and keep it to yourself. Then your world will be as you want it (if you don't keep going back in forth believing this and then believing that). Just stick to what you desire, imagine it and live in it. It's soothing, peaceful to do so, and yes never fails. This is how to get unlimited amounts of all you want! This is Extra surplus of happiness, power, money and it is Extra easy to do so. Don't be fooled by this technique's simplicity, as life is not to be as complex as our agile brain can make it seem. We get what we constantly imagine as true everyday anyway. Let's direct it to what we want. Let all your spoken words support the truth of your desire. Don't dare speak against it. It always works for me as long as I don't imagine the opposite. I stick to one script and enjoy the many great results. Oh and natural feeling and natural focus as though it is 'naturally' true is the ultimate form of imagination and works the fastest and keeps it exact. Always do it out of LOVE and in a perfect way so you don't get a warped version of what you want.Imagine as though you are living in a tv show of your exact liking and daily

experiencing it as if you believe that All things are possible. Get into it!!
See I begged and cried and still never got what I wanted

except more of what I was complaining about. I was the one imagining it that way and therefore making it a physical reality. Now I ignore the negative as though it is a gross lie and tell myself boldly and moment by moment that it is precisely as

good as I want it.
I know the mean people are extra nice and the broke people are actually very well off financially.

My whole world is fixed how I see fit. I imagine out of love and I get good to them and more good to me. Believe it like actors in a good movie are fully into their role each scene and feel it deeply as when you are watching that movie. This movie is called 'your life, your world'. Live in the experience you choose to go along with and let these unsatisfactory surroundings go away from your awareness. Just keep aware your life has all you want and enjoy and it will fill in the blank and become fully real as it has to; its nature. This is not a trick this is just how it is and now you know; so practice, prove it to yourself, live this and enjoy and pass it on. You probably know most things in life, so this technique is Extra and the only technique you need. Enjoy.

www.ingramcontent.com/pod-product-compliance
Lightning Source LLC
Chambersburg PA
CBHW081704220526
45466CB00009B/2880